What's My Role?

Colleen Hord

Educational Media

rourkeeducationalmedia.com

Scan for Related Titles
and Teacher Resources

www.rourkeeducationalmedia.com

PHOTO CREDITS: Cover: © Nytumbleweeds; Title Page: © Mari; Page 3: © JBryson; Page 5: Cathy Yeulet; Page 7: © Abdul Sami Haqqani; Page 9: © PenelopeB; Page 11: © ktaylorg; Page 13: © jgroup; Page 15: © Pavel Losevsky; Page 16: © Greg Epperson; Page 17: © Igor Vorobyov; Page 18: © CraigRJD; Page 19: © Kontrec; Page 21: © Natalya Korolevskaya; Page 22: © CraigRJD, Daniel Korzeniewski, Anthony Aneese Totah Jr.; Page 23: © PenelopeB, Cathy Yeulet, JBryson

Edited by: Meg Greve

Cover design by Tara Ramo
Interior design by Teri Intzegian

Library of Congress Cataloging-in-Publication Data

Hord, Colleen
 What's My Role? / Colleen Hord.
    p. cm. -- (Little World Social Studies)
 Includes bibliographical references and index.
 ISBN 978-1-61741-794-8 (hard cover - English) (alk. paper)
 ISBN 978-1-61741-996-6 (soft cover - English)
 ISBN 978-1-61236-712-5 (e-Book - English)
 ISBN 978-1-63430-137-4 (hard cover - Spanish)
 ISBN 978-1-63430-163-3 (soft cover - Spanish)
 ISBN 978-1-63430-189-3 (e-Book - Spanish)
 Library of Congress Control Number: 2011925064

Rourke Educational Media
Printed in the United States of America,
North Mankato, Minnesota

Also Available as:

rourkeeducationalmedia.com

customerservice@rourkeeducationalmedia.com • PO Box 643328 Vero Beach, Florida 32964

Have you ever wondered if you can make a difference to others?

Well, you can! You can make a difference in the **roles** you play at home, at school, and in your **community**.

Your role is to be **responsible** and caring wherever you are.

At home, you make a difference when you do your **chores** and when you are kind to family members.

Your role at school is to follow the school rules, and be helpful to your classmates and teachers.

You make a difference at school by playing with someone who doesn't have anyone else to play with, and by listening to your teachers.

Did You Know?

Boy Scouts and Girls Scouts are after school clubs. Boys and girls learn leadership skills and donate their time to help others.

You can make a difference in your community when you **volunteer**.

Volunteers give time and help to others.

You can be a volunteer in your community by visiting older people or by picking up **litter**.

Can you think of other ways you can volunteer?

Did You Know?

Habitat for Humanity is a group of people of all ages who volunteer their time and supplies to build houses for people who don't have them.

You don't have to be an adult to make a difference. You can make a difference right now!

Picture Glossary

 **chores** (CHORS): Small jobs like making your bed or taking out the trash are called chores.

 **community** (kuh-MYOO-nuh-tee): A place where a group of people live, work and care for each other.

 **litter** (LIT-ur): Trash or garbage, such as old papers, food scraps, or empty cans left on the ground is called litter.

responsible (ri-SPON-suh-buhl): People who are responsible are sensible and can be trusted.

roles (ROLES): Your expected behaviors of being responsible and caring at home, school, or in your community.

volunteer (VOL-uhn-tihr): Someone who offers to do a job without pay.

Index

Websites

www.kidskorps.org
www.habitat.org/youthprograms
www.slp.kiwanis.org/kkids/home.aspx

About the Author

Colleen Hord lives on a small farm with her husband, llamas, chickens, and cats. She enjoys kayaking, camping, walking on the beach, and reading to her grandchildren.

Meet The Author!
www.meetREMauthors.com

24